INSIDE THE NFL
NFC NORTH

THE CHICAGO BEARS
THE DETROIT LIONS
THE GREEN BAY PACKERS
THE MINNESOTA VIKINGS

BY K. C. KELLEY

The Child's World®

Published in the United States of America by
The Child's World® • 1980 Lookout Drive
Mankato, MN 56003-1705

800-599-READ • www.childsworld.com

ACKNOWLEDGEMENTS

The Child's World®: Mary Berendes,
Publishing Director

The Design Lab: Kathleen Petelinsek,
Design; Gregory Lindholm, Page Production

Manuscript consulting and photo research
by Shoreline Publishing Group LLC.

Thanks to Bob Woods and Jim Gigliotti for their
assistance with this book.

PHOTOS

Cover: Joe Robbins (2)
Interior: AP/Wide World: 5, 6, 8, 13, 14, 18, 23,
24, 27, 30; Joe
Robbins: 11, 12, 19, 20, 26, 29, 32.

LIBRARY OF CONGRESS
CATALOGING-IN-PUBLICATION DATA

Kelley, K. C.
  NFC North / by K.C. Kelley.
    p. cm. — (Inside the NFL)
  Includes bibliographical references and index.
  ISBN 978-1-59296-998-2
(library bound : alk. paper)
  1. National Football League—History—Juvenile
literature. 2. Football—United States—History—
Juvenile literature. I. Title. II. Series.
  GV955.5.N35K453 2008
  796.332'640973—dc22   2008010516

NFC NORTH
INTRODUCTION

T he NFL calls this division the National Football Conference (NFC) North. But to long-time football fans, the collection of teams including the Chicago Bears, Detroit Lions, Green Bay Packers, and Minnesota Vikings always will be known unofficially as the "Black-and-Blue Division."

That's because, since 1970, these four teams have waged fierce, hard-hitting battles twice each season for **supremacy** in their division. From 1970 to 2001, the division was called the NFC Central, and for a time these teams were joined by the Tampa Bay Buccaneers. When the NFL underwent a major **realignment** in 2002, the Buccaneers shifted to the NFC South, and the remaining four teams formed the new NFC North.

Now, strap on your pads, lace up your cleats, and tighten your chinstrap. We're going to tackle the "Black-and-Blue Division." We promise, though, it won't leave any bruises.

There's a reason why it's nicknamed the "Black-and-Blue Division"! The hits come hard—and often—among these long-time **rivals**.

CHAPTER ONE

THE CHICAGO BEARS

ronko Nagurski. Dick Butkus. Mike Singletary. Brian Urlacher. Even the names alone call to mind images of rugged, hard-nosed players. And that is the image of the Chicago Bears' player. Every NFL team seems to have its own **identity.** In Chicago, the Bears' identity is one of tough, defensive-minded football. It is reflected in the **franchise's** nickname: "The Monsters of the Midway."

Of course, the Bears have had some very good players on the offensive side of the ball, too. Chicago has featured a couple of the best running backs in NFL history in Walter Payton and Gale Sayers. Other Pro Football Hall of Famers on offense included quarterback Sid Luckman and tight end Mike Ditka.

Still, it is defense for which this club is known. It is defense, too, that has mostly carried the club

That's "Papa Bear," George Halas (left), with quarterback Sid Luckman.

to nine NFL championships (second only to the Green Bay Packers' 12 titles).

The Bears' first championship came in 1921, when they were known as the Chicago Staleys. The team was named after A.E. Staley, who owned a company in Decatur, Illinois, called the Staley Starch Works. He founded the Bears as original members of the NFL (which was then called the American **Professional** Football Association) in 1920 and placed the team in nearby Decatur. After one season, he sold the team to George Halas, who was a player as well as the head coach. Halas moved the Staleys to Chicago in 1921. He renamed the team the Bears in 1922.

Halas was one of the most influential figures in NFL history. He helped shape the nature of the league with many of his ideas. As a coach, he was the first to have his players practice every day. And he was the first coach to study game films of the Bears' opponents. As an owner, he was the first to put his team's games on the radio. And he was the first to organize publicity tours in nearby cities.

Perhaps Halas' most important contribution, though, was teaming with Boston (later Washington) owner George Preston Marshall to split the NFL into two divisions in 1933. That meant the winner of the two divisions would play in an **annual** championship game. That was the **forerunner** to the **Super Bowl.**

Halas got the idea when the final game of the 1932 season, between the Bears and the Portsmouth Spartans, decided the league title.

With quarterback Sid Luckman directing the Bears' famed T-Formation offense, Chicago won four league championships in the 1940s.

Chicago won that game, which was forced indoors because of a blizzard, 9–0. It was the Bears' second championship. Halas wanted a season-ending game to generate that kind of excitement every year.

Halas also knew how superstars could generate interest in his team and in the NFL, which was still very young. In 1925, the Bears signed one of the NFL's first superstars, Red Grange. A gifted runner, the "Galloping Ghost" also played defense. He drew huge crowds everywhere, which increased the NFL's popularity.

The Bears fielded other greats during that era. Paddy Driscoll could run, pass, catch, and particularly kick the football. His specialty, the **dropkick,** won many games. Bronko Nagurski, a rugged fullback and linebacker, powered the team to **consecutive** NFL championships in 1932 and 1933. The following year, his sensational blocking was his best weapon. Nagurski paved the way for Beattie Feathers to become the league's first 1,000-yard rusher (1,004). The Bears went undefeated, 13–0.

Chicago literally slipped up in the NFL title game, though, against the New York Giants in 1934. Playing on an ice-covered field at New York's Polo Grounds, the Bears led at halftime, 10–3. In the second half, the Giants switched from cleats to basketball shoes for better traction. New York rallied to win the famous "Sneakers Game," 30–13.

In the 1930s, Halas hired a famous college coach named Clark Shaughnessy to help out with the Bears. Shaughnessy's job was to show the Bears how to run the new T-Formation. In the T-Formation, the center snapped the ball directly to the quarterback, and three backs lined up behind the quarterback (so it looked as if all the players formed a "T").

The "T" took the NFL by storm. With future Pro Football Hall of Fame quarterback Sid Luckman running the offense, the Bears went 8–3 in 1940. They wiped out the Washington Redskins, 73–0, in the championship game. That remains the most lopsided game in NFL history.

It was also the first of the Bears' four straight trips to the title game; they were champs again in 1941, 1943, and 1946. By the 1950s, every NFL team was utilizing the T-Formation in some form. And it remains the basis for most offensive formations today.

The Bears produced another generation of stars in the 1960s. They helped the team win it all in 1963. Tight end Mike Ditka was a sure-handed receiver and a hard-nosed blocker. Dick Butkus often is considered the best middle linebacker ever. Later, running back Gale Sayers scored 22 touchdowns as a **rookie** in 1965—including six in one game! These three players were the core of the team in 1967, the last year Halas coached. (In all, he coached 40 years in four separate 10-year periods.)

Over the next decade, the Bears went into hibernation. They didn't have a winning season again until 1977, when they made the **playoffs** as a wild-card team. They got that far in 1979, too, but both times were ousted in the first game.

In 1982, Halas brought Ditka back to be the head coach of the Bears. By 1985, "Iron Mike" had forged a team in his own image: tough, in-your-face defense; run-oriented, grind-it-out offense. The stars were running back Walter Payton, linebacker Mike Singletary, and 300-pound (136-kilogram) defensive tackle William "Refrigerator" Perry. The Bears' fearsome "46" defense was designed to stuff the run and blitz the quarterback. Sometimes they stacked eight pass rushers near the **line of scrimmage.**

Chicago went 15–1 that season, then blanked the Giants (21–0) and the Rams (24–0) in the playoffs. In Super Bowl XX, the Bears stomped the New England Patriots 46–10. Their win included a one-yard touchdown dive by the "Fridge," who lined up as a fullback.

The Bears' Devin Hester is an amazing kick returner. No player in NFL history had ever returned 5 kicks for touchdowns in one season until Hester returned three punts and two kickoffs for scores in 2006. Then, he brought back four punts and two kickoffs for scores to break his own record in 2007.

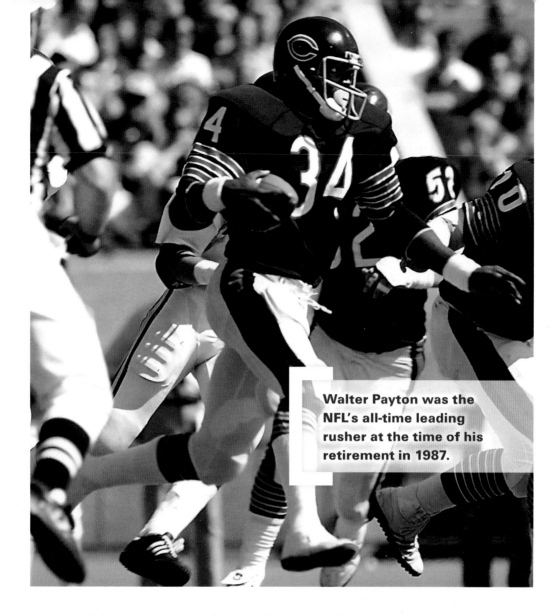

Walter Payton was the NFL's all-time leading rusher at the time of his retirement in 1987.

The Bears remained Central Division champs the next three years, but saw only one playoff victory in that span. Then they were up and down in the 1990s.

Following a terrible 2000 season (5–11), Chicago had a great year in 2001. The Bears finished the regular season 13–3 behind a typically tough defense, starring middle linebacker Brian Urlacher, and an efficient offense. But the Bears fell to the Philadelphia Eagles in the first game of the playoffs, then stumbled to losing records each of the next two seasons.

The Bears' defense helped carry the club to the Super Bowl in the 2006 season, but Peyton Manning (18) and the Colts won the game.

In 2004, Chicago brought in Lovie Smith to coach the team. Smith was the man who built aggressive defenses as the coordinator in Tampa Bay and St. Louis. His influence was evident from the start. Chicago featured a ball-hawking defense and improved special-teams play in his first year. By his second year, the Bears were champions of the NFC North. And in his third season, in 2006, Chicago made it back to the Super Bowl.

The Bears lost that game to quarterback Peyton Manning and the Colts. Then they struggled through a tough 2007 season in which their own quarterback play was spotty. But clearly, they have shown the league that the "Monsters of the Midway" are still a force!

CHAPTER TWO
THE DETROIT LIONS

In recent years, the Detroit Lions have been a team in search of an identity—and their struggles have been reflected in **mediocre** won-lost records. But it has not always been that way. The Lions, whose franchise started play in 1930, were an NFL powerhouse in the 1950s, when they combined the leadership of a **swashbuckling** quarterback with a fierce, hard-hitting defense to win three league championships.

The Lions' franchise began play in Portsmouth, Ohio, in 1930. Like many other clubs at the time, they started out as a "town team" in the small community. The team was called the Portsmouth Spartans.

In four seasons in Portsmouth, the club had some success on the field, although little at the gate. Still, the Spartans left their mark

Quarterback Earl "Dutch" Clark was one of the club's earliest stars.

Here is what football looked like in the 1930s. That is Detroit's Dutch Clark with the ball in a game against the Cleveland Rams in 1938.

on pro football by playing in one of the most important games in NFL history. It came in 1932, when the Spartans and the Chicago Bears tied atop the league standings at the end of the regular season. Because there was no playoff system at the time, the teams agreed to play one more game in Chicago to break the tie and determine the NFL champion.

On the day of the game, there was a huge blizzard. The game couldn't be played outdoors. So the teams agreed to move it indoors to Chicago Stadium, which was the home of hockey's Chicago Black Hawks. The field in Chicago Stadium was shorter and narrower. To keep the players from running into the hockey boards, the ball was placed closer to the middle of the field after each play. The idea made so much sense that it led to permanent "hashmarks"—the two rows of short white lines in the middle of the field where the ball is spotted for each snap—beginning with the next season's games.

Portsmouth lost that game 9–0, and the Bears were the champions. But the idea of a season-ending championship game like that was so appealing to NFL owners that they split the league into two divisions beginning in 1933. Thus, the NFL Championship Game—the forerunner to the Super Bowl—was born.

In 1934, a Detroit radio executive named George Richards purchased the Spartans' franchise, moved it to Detroit, and named it the Lions.

The early Lions' teams had some very good players, but none better than Dutch Clark. He was an All-NFL quarterback, but he also ran the ball, kicked, and played defensive back. Clark propelled Detroit's new team to victory in its first 10 games. But by losing the final three, the Lions finished in second place.

Two of those losses were to their Western Division rivals, the Bears. The first came on Thanksgiving, which began an NFL tradition of the Lions hosting a Turkey Day game every year. (The most famous of Detroit's Thanksgiving games came in 1962 against the Packers, who arrived at Tiger Stadium with a perfect 10–0 record. They left with their only loss of that season. The Lions'

In their first season in Detroit in 1934, the Lions got off to an unbelievable start. They shut out each of their first seven opponents and did not lose until their 11th game.

ferocious defensive line—Darris McCord, Alex Karras, Roger Brown, and Sam Williams—sacked Bart Starr 11 times in Detroit's 26–14 victory.)

The Lions won their first NFL championship in 1935 behind a strong running game. Three Lions were among the NFL's top five rushers: Ernie Caddell, Clark, and Bill Shepherd.

The team posted winning records from 1936 to 1939, but only two over the next 10 seasons. Still, they fielded some memorable players, including a pair of Hall of Famers: halfback Bill Dudley and center-linebacker Alex Wojciechowicz. There was also Byron "Whizzer" White, a "triple threat" (passing, rushing, punting). He stayed only two seasons and eventually became a U.S. Supreme Court Justice.

The 1950s were fabulous for the Lions. The team was loaded with stars. On offense were quarterback Bobby Layne, running back Doak Walker, and guard-tackle Lou Creekmur. Layne didn't have the strongest arm or the quickest feet, but he was a fearless leader who brought a swagger to the club. Walker once paid him the ultimate compliment for a quarterback: "Bobby never lost a game. Time simply ran out on him."

On defense, the Lions were led by safety Jack Christiansen and, beginning in 1953, linebacker Joe Schmidt. During the decade, Detroit won three NFL championships, in 1952, 1953, and 1957.

All three championships were gained in hard-fought title games against the tough Cleveland Browns. In the 1953 game, Layne engineered a

One of the most famous games in Detroit's history was a Western Conference playoff against the 49ers in 1957. After falling behind 27–7 in the third quarter, the Lions roared back for a 31–27 victory that sent them to the NFL title game.

Doak Walker played only six years in the 1950s, but he was so good, he's in the Pro Football Hall of Fame.

nail-biting, game-winning drive in the final minutes. With 2:08 left, he connected with Jim Doran—who usually played defensive end— for a 33-yard touchdown to seal the 17–16 win.

The Lions assembled a great defense in the early 1960s. The top players were Schmidt, Yale Lary, and Dick "Night Train" Lane. However, that mighty crew couldn't quite overcome the powerful Packers. The Lions came in second to them three straight seasons,

Running back Barry Sanders wasn't the biggest player in professional football, but his statistics were huge.

1960 to 1962. In fact, from 1969 through 1975, a frustrated Detroit played the second-place "bridesmaid" role seven consecutive times. That final season also marked the team's move to the suburbs and the Pontiac Silverdome.

The Lions finally got over the hump and won the NFC Central Division in 1983—only to lose a 24–23 heartbreaker to the 49ers in the first playoff game. During the 1988 season, after too many losing seasons, owner William Clay Ford (grandson of Henry Ford) named Wayne Fontes head coach. Fontes used a fast-paced, **Run-and-Shoot offense** that the Lions called the "Silver Stretch."

With superstar running back Barry Sanders and speedy wide receivers, Detroit streaked to a 12–4, division-winning season in 1991. The Lions lost the NFC Championship Game to the Redskins, the eventual Super Bowl XXVI winners.

The phenomenal Sanders—only 5 feet 8 inches (173 centimeters) tall and 200 pounds (91 kg)—piled up rushing yards throughout the 1990s. He was the NFL's leading rusher in 1990, 1994, 1996, and 1997. He captured his third rushing title with a dramatic, 175-yard outburst on the final Monday night of the season in San Francisco. In 1997, Sanders became only the third player in NFL history to rush for more than 2,000 yards (2,053) in a season. To the fans' dismay, he suddenly retired after the 1998 campaign.

The Lions were in the playoffs six times during the 1990s, but came away with only a single victory. In fact, that win over the Cowboys in the 1991 divisional playoffs is the only **postseason** win for the club since its 1957 championship.

That's been a long drought. The Lions haven't even been to the playoffs in the 2000s. The 2007 season was particularly disappointing. Detroit bolted from the gate, winning six of its first eight games and looking like a genuine playoff team behind the inspired play of quarterback Jon Kitna and star wide receiver Roy Williams. But a disastrous six-game losing streak followed, and Detroit missed out on the postseason again.

From 1975 to 2001, the Lions played their home games in the Silverdome in nearby Pontiac, Michigan. In 2002, they moved back to Detroit to play in that city's brand-new Ford Field.

CHAPTER THREE

THE GREEN BAY PACKERS

Football fans are crazy for their Packers in Green Bay. And why shouldn't they be? With 12 championships, the Packers have won more league titles than any other NFL team. But Green Bay's appeal goes far beyond just wins and losses. The Packers are a small-market team that has been an important part of the community for almost 90 years. The club is the only publicly owned franchise in the NFL.

The Packers' ties to the community go all the way back to 1919. The club began that year when co-founder Earl "Curly" Lambeau talked his employer at the Indian Packing Company into donating $500 for uniforms and equipment. That's how the team got the name "Packers."

After a couple of seasons, the Packers joined the NFL (then called the American Professional Football

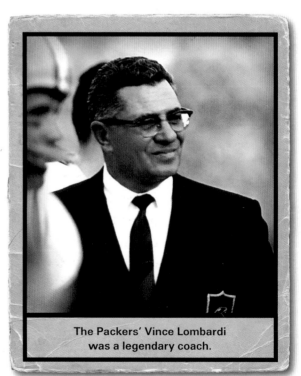

The Packers' Vince Lombardi was a legendary coach.

Association) in 1921, the league's second year. After missing a year in 1922 because of rules violations, the club became a **publicly held company** and returned to the NFL for good in 1923. It's been a terrific ride ever since.

The Packers first served notice that they were an NFL force in 1929. After several good, but not great, seasons, Green Bay went undefeated that year with Lambeau as coach. Their 12–0–1 record earned them the first of three consecutive league championships.

Leaders of the original "Pack" were some of the game's earliest superstars. These players included tailback Arnie Herber, tackle Cal Hubbard, and Johnny "Blood" McNally. New blood arrived over the next few years, including fullback Clarke Hinkle and receiver Don Hutson. All of them are now in the Pro Football Hall of Fame.

The Packers claimed another NFL title in 1936. They lost to the Giants in the 1938 championship game, but shut out New York a year later, 27–0, to earn the franchise's fifth title.

Green Bay bettered its New York rivals again in 1944. That title game was dominated by fullback Ted Fritsch. He scored both touchdowns in the Packers' 14–7 triumph. Then began a long drought. From 1945 to 1959, the Packers finished no better than third place. Fortunately, better days were to come.

Vince Lombardi was hired as coach and **general manager** in 1959. He inherited a squad loaded with future Hall of Famers. The stars were quarterback Bart Starr, fullback Jim Taylor, halfback Paul Hornung, tackle Forrest Gregg, and center Jim Ringo. Green Bay went 7–5 in Lombardi's first year. It was the team's first winning season since 1947.

The Packers lost the championship game in 1960, Lombardi's only playoff defeat. Taylor ran for 1,307 yards in 1961, and Green Bay won the West again. The Packers shut out the Giants 37–0 in the title game. After a 13–1 finish in 1962, Green Bay edged New York 16–7 for another title.

In 1965, Baltimore and Green Bay ended with identical 10–3–1 records, forcing a playoff game. Don Chandler's field goal was the difference in the Packers' 13–10 win. The title game was played on a cold, snow- and mud-drenched Lambeau Field. Green Bay held Cleveland's bruising fullback, Jim Brown, to 50 yards. Meanwhile, Taylor and Hornung combined to gain 201 yards, and the home team prevailed, 23–12.

Two more consecutive NFL championships netted trips to Super Bowls I and II to play the winners of the rival American Football League (AFL). In the 1966 season, Green Bay scored three second-half touchdowns to topple the Kansas City Chiefs, 35–10. Super Bowl II, versus the Oakland Raiders, featured another second-half surge and a 33–14 Packers' victory. That turned out to be Lombardi's last game in "Titletown."

Several coaches, including Starr and Gregg, tried—but failed—to rekindle the Lombardi magic. Except for playoff appearances in 1972 and

In the 1940s, the Packers' Don Hutson stood head and shoulders above all other pass catchers. Take 1942, for instance. He set an NFL record by catching 74 passes (including 17 for touchdowns). The next player on the receiving chart that year had only 27 receptions.

Running back Donny Anderson (44) scored a touchdown on this play against the Oakland Raiders during Super Bowl II.

1982, the Packers were mediocre until the early 1990s. Head coach Mike Holmgren, an offensive guru from the 49ers, came to town in 1992, along with quarterback Brett Favre.

Favre was a backup in Atlanta his rookie season in 1991, but the Packers sent a first-round draft pick to the Falcons to acquire him. It turned out to be a steal. Favre came off the bench in the third game of 1992 and rallied the club to a victory against Cincinnati

Quarterback Brett Favre had reason to celebrate while leading the Packers over the Patriots in Super Bowl XXXI.

with a touchdown pass in the last minute. The Packers found their quarterback. Favre started every game for the team all the way until his retirement at the end of the 2007 season.

Fearless in the **pocket,** the cannon-armed Favre and receiver Sterling Sharpe helped Green Bay to the playoffs in 1993. The Packers won wild-card games that year and the next. By 1995, a defense sparked by hulking end Reggie White slammed the brakes on opponents. The 11–5 Packers dethroned the reigning NFL-champion 49ers in the second playoff game. In the NFC title game against Dallas, however, they ran out of gas in the fourth quarter and lost.

The Pack was back in 1996, as Favre earned his second of three straight trophies as the league's most valuable player. A dominant 13–3 regular season ended with a 35–21 victory over New England in Super Bowl XXXI. It was Green Bay's first NFL title since 1967.

The Packers were regulars in the playoffs for nearly a decade after that, even after Holmgren stepped down following the 1998 season. They returned to the Super Bowl in 1997 (losing a close decision to Denver), and missed the postseason only twice from 1993 to 2004. Beginning in 2002, they won the first three NFC North titles.

Shockingly, though, Green Bay fell to a last-place finish in 2005. Mike McCarthy, a noted NFL offensive assistant, was brought in as head coach in '06. But the Packers missed the playoffs again. At 37, it appeared that Favre would never again be the quarterback he once was.

Then, Favre seemed to turn back the clock in 2007. Green Bay had the youngest team in the league that season, and Favre played like one of the kids. On offense, emerging stars such as wide receiver Greg Jennings and running back Ryan Grant teamed with veterans such as Favre and receiver Donald Driver. On defense, pass-rushing end Aaron Kampman and cornerback Al Harris made the Pro Bowl.

Favre passed for 4,157 yards (his most since 1998) and 28 touchdowns, and Green Bay was the surprise team of the NFL. The Packers won 13 games during the regular season.

Brett Favre played his last season in 2007—and it was one of his best. The Packers were the surprise team of the NFL that year.

A close loss to the New York Giants in the NFC title game ended Green Bay's Super Bowl hopes. Then, after 17 NFL seasons, Favre retired. The Packers began a new era in 2008 with Aaron Rodgers, a first-round draft pick in 2005, trying to follow in Favre's footsteps.

CHAPTER FOUR

THE MINNESOTA VIKINGS

There is a word to describe a pleasurable experience that is mixed with a bit of sadness. It is called "bittersweet"— and it is a good way to describe the feelings that Minnesota Vikings' fans have had while rooting for their team through the years. The team's history is filled with many winning seasons and memorable moments. But the club has been foiled in several good chances to take the NFL's ultimate prize: the Super Bowl.

The Vikings are the youngest franchise in the NFC North. They began their existence as an NFL **expansion team** in 1961. From their very first game, though, they proved they could compete with the league's established teams. And by the end of their first decade, the Vikings were NFL champions.

Minnesota's first game was on September 17, 1961. The Vikings

Head coach Bud Grant (center) helped the Vikings become big winners.

hosted the powerful Chicago Bears that day. The big, bad Bears had been in the league for 40 years already and had seven NFL championships under their shoulder pads.

That didn't matter to the Vikings, a mix of **expansion draft** veterans and raw rookies. One of the youngsters was an unexpected star that Sunday afternoon. Quarterback Fran Tarkenton came off the bench and passed for four touchdowns and **scrambled** for another. The 37–13 victory upset Chicago, but thrilled the more than 32,000 Vikings fans who packed Metropolitan Stadium in Minneapolis.

Minnesota won only two more games during its first season. Meanwhile, head coach Norm Van Brocklin was nurturing his young team. With Tarkenton under center, halfback Tommy Mason and fullback Bill Brown in the backfield, Paul Flatley at wide receiver, and Carl Eller at defensive end, the "Vikes" achieved their first winning season (8–5–1) in 1964.

But Van Brocklin and Tarkenton didn't always get along, and both departed following a disappointing 1966 season (4–9–1). Down came Bud Grant, head coach of the Canadian Football League's Winnipeg Blue Bombers, and up went the Vikings' fortunes. Grant developed a cast of talented rookies: defensive tackle Alan Page, wide receiver Gene Washington, running back Clint Jones, and defensive backs Bobby Bryant and Bob Grim. He also recruited quarterback Joe Kapp, who was his quarterback in Winnipeg.

Minnesota's defensive linemen grabbed most of the headlines, but safety Paul Krause was another star for the Vikings' defense from 1968 to 1979. He posted 53 of his NFL-record 81 career interceptions while playing for Minnesota.

Quarterback Fran Tarkenton (10) was definitely a great passer, but he could run well, too.

Kapp and company captured the Central Division title in 1968, but lost to Baltimore in the Vikings' first postseason game. Minnesota ruled the "Black and Blue" in 1969, going 12–2, then won two home playoff games to capture their only NFL championship. In Super Bowl IV, the Vikings lost 23–7 to the AFL's Kansas City Chiefs. (The next year, the AFL and the NFL officially became one league.)

The NFL's revolving door brought Tarkenton back to Minnesota from the Giants in 1972, though the team only managed a .500

finish. The Vikings enjoyed a division-best 12–2 record in 1973, which began an incredible streak of six straight Central Division titles. Minnesota won the NFC title in '73 and played in Super Bowl VIII, which it lost to the Dolphins, 24–7.

During that period, the defense's "Purple People Eaters" devoured opponents. The nickname was for Minnesota's powerful **front four:** Eller, Page, Gary Larsen, and Jim Marshall. Whether it was sacking the quarterback, tackling a ball carrier for a loss, or batting down a pass, the Purple People Eaters were relentless.

In 1974, Minnesota advanced to its third Super Bowl, only to be turned away this time by the Steelers. After another 12–2 season in 1975, the Vikings dropped their first playoff game to Dallas on Roger Staubach's 50-yard desperation pass to Drew Pearson with 24 seconds left. Grant guided his squad to a fourth Super Bowl in 1976, but they were beaten by the Oakland Raiders.

The Vikings returned to the playoffs the next two seasons, but failed to reach the Super Bowl. By then, too, the Purple People Eaters' reign of terror was over.

Following playoff runs in 1980 and 1982, Grant retired after the 1983 season—Minnesota's second in the Metrodome. The team slumped to 3–13 in 1984. Grant came back for the 1985 season, then turned over the reins to long-time assistant Jerry Burns.

Burns produced three playoff teams, the last during the 1989 season when the Vikings and the Cowboys pulled off a megadeal. In a trade involving 18 players and draft picks, Minnesota acquired former Heisman Trophy-winning running back Herschel Walker from Dallas. However, ill-suited to the Vikings' offense, Walker went to the Eagles two years later.

By the mid-1990s, Minnesota possessed a potent passing game. The Vikings obtained former Houston Oilers quarterback Warren Moon, who meshed with wide receivers Jake Reed, Qadry Ismail, and Cris Carter. Dennis Green, who replaced Burns as coach in 1992, pushed the team to the playoffs his first three seasons but failed to win a postseason game.

In fact, the Vikings' next playoff victory was a shocker against the Giants in 1997. Trailing 22–13 in the fourth quarter, Minnesota scored 10 points in 90 seconds for a miraculous win. The season ended with a divisional-playoff loss at San Francisco the following week.

It looked as if the Vikings might end their Super Bowl drought in 1998. The team was dominant during the regular season, winning 15 of 16 games. Quarterback Randall Cunningham passed for 3,704 yards and 34 touchdowns. Wide receivers Cris Carter and Randy Moss were a strong one-two punch. Running back Robert Smith gained 1,187 yards on the ground. And kicker Gary Anderson didn't miss a single try. He made all 39 of his field-goal attempts and all 59 extra points.

In the playoffs, Minnesota rolled past Arizona 41–21 in the divisional round. Then, with the team leading Atlanta in the fourth quarter of the NFC title game, Anderson, unbelievably, missed a field-goal try. The Falcons tied the game with a late touchdown pass, then won it in **overtime.**

A fresh generation of superstars powered the Vikings into the new century. Daunte Culpepper represented the new-age quarterback: big, powerful, mobile, and strong-armed. He was complemented by Moss, whose leaping ability and running after a catch made the duo dynamic. Yet back-to-back playoff collapses in 1999 and 2000 were followed by several mediocre seasons. Culpepper and Moss were eventually traded away.

In 2004, Daunte Culpepper had one of the best seasons by a quarterback in NFL history. He passed for 4,717 yards and 39 touchdowns. His passer rating was 110.9—the fourth-best mark at the time.

Running back Adrian Peterson burst onto the scene as a rookie in 2007. In one game against San Diego, he rushed for an NFL-record 296 yards.

In 2006, the Vikings brought in former Philadelphia Eagles offensive coordinator Brad Childress as coach. And then, in 2007, the club made the move that its fans hope may one day bring a Super Bowl title to Minnesota. The club selected former Oklahoma running back Adrian Peterson with the seventh overall pick in the draft. Peterson's powerful running and a good defense kept the Vikings in the playoff chase until the final weekend of the season.

Although the year ended with back-to-back losses that cost Minnesota a postseason spot, the Vikings had served notice that they were still one of the NFL's most explosive and exciting teams.

ME LINE

1920
American Professional Football Association founded, with Decatur Staleys (later Chicago Bears) as one of its first members; league changed its name to the National Football League in 1922

1921
Green Bay Packers join league; Staleys win title

1929
Packers win first of three straight league titles

1933
Bears win first NFL Championship Game over New York Giants

1934
Portsmouth team moves to Detroit and takes the name Lions

20   1930   1940   1950   1960

1933
Bears win first NFL Championship Game over New York Giants

1934
Portsmouth team moves to Detroit and takes the name Lions

1940
Bears set a record by defeating Washington 73–0 to win NFL championship; they also won the league in 1941, 1943, and 1946

1952
Detroit wins first of two straight league titles; they would win again in 1957

1961
Green Bay wins NFL championship, first of five it would win in the decade; Minnesota Vikings play first season in NFL, finishing 3–11

1966
Green Bay wins first AFL-NFL Championship Game, later called Super Bowl I, by beating the Kansas City Chiefs

1967
Packers beat the Oakland Raiders for their second Super Bowl victory in a row

1969
Vikings earn berth in Super Bowl IV, first of four Super Bowls the team would play in (and lose)

1970   **1980**   **1990**   **2000**   **2010**

1985
Chicago wins Super Bowl XX

1996
Packers win Super Bowl XXXI; they would lose in Super Bowl XXXII the next season

2006
Bears win their first NFC title in 21 years, but fall to the Indianapolis Colts in Super Bowl XLI

STAT STUFF

TEAM RECORDS (THROUGH 2007)

	All-time Record	Number of Titles (Most Recent)	Number of Times in Playoffs	Top Coach (Wins)
...go	693–508–42	9 (1985)	24	George Halas (324)
...t	495–563–32	4 (1957)	14	Wayne Fontes (67)
...Bay	662–518–36	12 (1996)	24	Curly Lambeau (212)
...sota	403–340–9	1 (1969)	24	Bud Grant (168)

NFC NORTH CAREER LEADERS (THROUGH 2007)

Category	Name (Years With Team)	Total
Chicago		
Rushing yards	Walter Payton (1975–1987)	16,726
Passing yards	Sid Luckman (1939–1950)	14,686
Touchdown passes	Sid Luckman (1939–1950)	137
Receptions	Walter Payton (1975–1987)	492
Touchdowns	Walter Payton (1975–1987)	125
Scoring	Kevin Butler (1985–1995)	1,116
Detroit		
Rushing yards	Barry Sanders (1989–1998)	15,269
Passing yards	Bobby Layne (1950–1958)	15,710
Touchdown passes	Bobby Layne (1950–1958)	118
Receptions	Herman Moore (1991–2001)	670
Touchdowns	Barry Sanders (1989–1998)	109
Scoring	Jason Hanson (1992–2007)	1,659
Green Bay		
Rushing yards	Jim Taylor (1958–1966)	8,207
Passing yards	Brett Favre (1992–2007)	61,657
Touchdown passes	Brett Favre (1992–2007)	442
Receptions	Sterling Sharpe (1988–1994)	595
Touchdowns	Don Hutson (1935–1945)	105
Scoring	Ryan Longwell (1997–2005)	1,054
Minnesota		
Rushing yards	Robert Smith (1993–2000)	6,818
Passing yards	Fran Tarkenton (1961–66, 1972–78)	33,098
Touchdown passes	Fran Tarkenton (1961–66, 1972–78)	239
Receptions	Cris Carter (1990–2001)	1,004
Touchdowns	Cris Carter (1990–2001)	110
Scoring	Fred Cox (1963–1977)	1,365

MEMBERS OF THE PRO FOOTBALL HALL OF FAME

Player	Position	Date Inducted
Chicago		
Doug Atkins	Defensive End	1982
George Blanda	Quarterback/Kicker	1981
Dick Butkus	Linebacker	1979
Guy Chamberlin	End/Coach	1965
George Connor	Tackle	1975
Jimmy Conzelman	Quarterback/Coach	1964
Mike Ditka	Tight End	1988
John "Paddy" Driscoll	Quarterback	1965
Jim Finks	General Manager	1995
Dan Fortmann	Guard	1965
Bill George	Linebacker	1974
Harold "Red" Grange	Halfback	1963
George Halas	Coach/Owner	1963
Dan Hampton	Defensive End	2002
Ed Healey	Tackle	1964
Bill Hewitt	Wide Receiver	1974
Stan Jones	Guard/Defensive Tackle	1991
Walt Kiesling	Guard/Coach	1966
Bobby Layne	Quarterback	1967
Sid Luckman	Quarterback	1965
William Roy "Link" Lyman	Tackle	1964
George McAfee	Halfback	1966
George Musso	Guard	1982
Bronko Nagurski	Fullback	1963
Alan Page	Defensive Tackle	1988
Walter Payton	Running Back	1993
Gale Sayers	Running Back	1977
Mike Singletary	Linebacker	1998
Joe Stydahar	Tackle	1967
George Trafton	Center	1964
Clyde "Bulldog" Turner	Center/Linebacker	1966
Detroit		
Lem Barney	Cornerback	1992
Jack Christiansen	Defensive End	1970
Earl "Dutch" Clark	Quarterback	1963
Lee Creekmur	Tackle/Guard	1996
Bill Dudley	Halfback	1966
Frank Gatski	Center	1985
John Henry Johnson	Fullback	1987
Dick "Night Train" Lane	Cornerback	1974
Yale Lary	Defensive Back	1979
Bobby Layne	Quarterback	1967
Ollie Matson	Halfback	1972
Hugh McElhenny	Halfback	1970
Barry Sanders	Running Back	2004
Charlie Sanders	Tight End	2007
Joe Schmidt	Linebacker	1973
Doak Walker	Halfback	1986
Alex Wojciechowicz	Center/Linebacker	1968

ORE STAT STUFF

MEMBERS OF THE PRO FOOTBALL HALL OF FAME

Player	Position	Date Inducted
Green Bay		
Herb Adderley	Cornerback	1980
Tony Canadeo	Halfback	1974
Willie Davis	Defensive End	1981
Len Ford	Defensive End	1976
Forrest Gregg	Tackle/Guard	1977
Ted Hendricks	Linebacker	1990
Arnie Herber	Quarterback	1966
Clarke Hinkle	Fullback	1964
Paul Hornung	Halfback	1986
Robert "Cal" Hubbard	Tackle	1963
Don Hutson	Wide Receiver	1963
Henry Jordan	Defensive Tackle	1995
Walt Kiesling	Guard/Coach	1966
Earl "Curly" Lambeau	Coach	1963
James Lofton	Wide Receiver	2003
Vince Lombardi	Coach	1971
John (Blood) McNally	Halfback	1963
Mike Michalske	Guard	1964
Ray Nitschke	Middle Linebacker	1978
Jim Ringo	Center	1981
Bart Starr	Quarterback	1977
Jan Stenerud	Kicker	1991
Jim Taylor	Fullback	1976
Emlen Tunnell	Safety	1967
Reggie White	Defensive End	2006
Willie Wood	Safety	1989
Minnesota		
Dave Casper	Tight End	2002
Carl Eller	Defensive End	2004
Jim Finks	General Manager	1995
Bud Grant	Coach	1994
Paul Krause	Safety	1998
Jim Langer	Center	1987
Hugh McElhenny	Halfback	1970
Warren Moon	Quarterback	2006
Alan Page	Defensive Tackle	1988
Jan Stenerud	Kicker	1991
Fran Tarkenton	Quarterback	1986
Ron Yary	Tackle	2001
Gary Zimmerman	Tackle	2008

GLOSSARY

annual—happening each year

consecutive—in a row

dropkick—a kick made by dropping the ball straight down and striking it just as it hits the ground; though still legal, it is hardly ever used

expansion draft—when a new team enters the NFL, older teams let the new team choose players from their rosters

expansion team—a new franchise that starts from scratch

forerunner—someone or something that prepares the way for someone or something else to follow

franchise—more than just the team, it is the entire organization that is a member of a professional sports league

front four—the defensive line

general manager—a person who runs the football team away from the field, helping to choose players and to organize the business

identity—the qualities or characteristics of a person or group

line of scrimmage—an imaginary line that goes from sideline to sideline at the spot where each play begins

mediocre—not really good, but not really bad; average

merger—the combining of two or more groups

overtime—a period of play after the regular time

playoffs—after the regular schedule, these are the games played to determine the champion

pocket—the space around a quarterback created by blockers as he tries to pass

postseason—the period in which the playoffs are held

professional—someone who is paid to perform an activity (in this case, play football)

publicly held company—a company that is owned by members of the public who have bought portions called "shares"

realignment—a change in the way a league organizes, or groups, its teams

rivals—people (or teams) who compete for the same goal

rookie—an athlete in his or her first season as a professional

Run-and-Shoot offense—a strategy that uses many short passes, quick runs, and few huddles

scrambled—when a quarterback ran, whether to buy time to find a receiver or to gain yards

Super Bowl—the NFL's yearly championship game, played in late January or early February at a different stadium each year

supremacy—ranking the highest

swashbuckling—acting in the manner of a swashbuckler; that is, with daring and adventure and aggressiveness

FIND OUT MORE

Books

Buckley, James Jr. *Eyewitness Super Bowl*. New York: DK Publishing, 2003.

Frisch, Aaron. *The History of the Detroit Lions*. Mankato, Minn.: Creative Education, 2004.

Frisch, Aaron. *The History of the Minnesota Vikings*. Mankato, Minn.: Creative Education, 2005.

Ladewski, Paul. *National Football League Superstars 2007*. New York: Scholastic, 2007.

Stewart, Mark. *The Chicago Bears*. Chicago: Norwood House Press, 2007.

Stewart, Mark. *The Green Bay Packers*. Chicago: Norwood House Press, 2007.

On the Web

Visit our Web site for lots of links about the NFC North:
http://www.childsworld.com/links

Note to Parents, Teachers, and Librarians: We routinely verify our Web links to make sure they are safe, active sites—so encourage your readers to check them out!

INDEX